LET US GO
TO BETHLEHEM!

LET US GO TO BETHLEHEM!
The First Christmas for Beginning Readers

Luke 2:1-20 FOR CHILDREN

by Dorothy Van Woerkom
illustrated by Aline Cunningham

I CAN READ A BIBLE STORY
Series Editor: Dorothy Van Woerkom

Publishing House
St. Louis

THIS IS ESPECIALLY FOR
CAROL GREENE

Concordia Publishing House, St. Louis, Missouri
Copyright © 1976 Concordia Publishing House

Library of Congress Cataloging in Publication Data

Van Woerkom, Dorothy.
    Let us go to Bethlehem!

    (I can read a Bible story)
    SUMMARY: Easy-to-read retelling of the birth of Jesus Christ.
    1. Jesus Christ—Nativity—Juvenile literature. [1. Jesus Christ—
Nativity] I. Cunningham, Aline. II. Title.
BT315.2.V34   226'.4'09505   76-14918
ISBN 0-570-07306-5
ISBN 0-570-07300-6 pbk.

Tap! Tap! Tap!
This was the sound of
Joseph's hammer
as he worked in his shop.

Joseph was a carpenter.
He lived a long time ago
in a little town called
Nazareth.

Each day when his work was done,

Joseph closed up his shop.

He hurried home to Mary,

his wife.

Each morning he

came back to work.

But today was
different.
Today Joseph closed his shop
and took his tools with him.
He would not come back to work
in the morning.
He had to go to Bethlehem.

Joseph was going to Bethlehem
to pay a tax.
He did not know how long
he would be away
from Nazareth.

Mary was going to Bethlehem, too.

She was getting food ready

for the trip.

She laid clean clothes out

near the fire.

Then she took a long white cloth
and folded it.
This cloth was for her baby
who would soon be born.

Morning came.

Joseph brought their donkey

to the door of the house.

He helped Mary climb up

on its back.

Joseph led the donkey slowly
down the hill—
away from home,
away from Nazareth.

The road to Bethlehem was long
and dusty.

There were many hills to climb.

The days were hot.

The nights were cold.

The stones hurt Joseph's feet.

For many miles,

Mary and Joseph were all alone

on the hilly road.

But sometimes they met people

passing by with noisy carts

and shouting children.

They were all going to Bethlehem.

Sometimes they met friends
who stopped to talk with them.
They often ate their meals
with other families
in the shade of a big rock.

One afternoon they rested
at the top of a hill.
"Look," Joseph said.
"There is Bethlehem!"

Mary looked.

There was the town,

on a hill not far away.

"It will be good

to sleep at the inn!" she said.

"Let's hurry, Joseph.

We are both very tired.

And so is this poor donkey."

Joseph led the donkey over the hill
to Bethlehem.

Bethlehem was a busy place.

Hundreds of people had come

to pay taxes.

Others had come to sell the things

they had made.

Some brought food to sell.

Joseph pushed his way to the door of the inn.

A man said to Joseph, "Go back. The inn is full. You will not find room here tonight."

But Joseph did not turn back.

He went into the inn.

"Please! he said to the innkeeper.

"We must have a place to stay.

We have come a long way,

and we are very tired."

The innkeeper looked sad.

"I wish I could help you," he said.

"But wait! Maybe I can."

He brought Mary and Joseph to a

cave behind the inn.

The innkeeper kept his oxen

and his donkey here.

The cave was warm.

The straw was clean,

and it smelled sweet.

Mary and Joseph decided to stay
in the cave.
They made beds for themselves
in the clean straw.

Joseph took the donkey's food
out of the manger.
He filled the manger with straw
to make a bed for the baby.

In a little while
Jesus was born.
Mary wound the long white cloth
around Him.
She laid Him in the manger.

It was night.

On a hill near Bethlehem
shepherds were watching
their sheep.

Suddenly an angel came to them.

There was a bright light
all around the angel.

The shepherds were afraid.

"Do not be afraid," the angel said.

"I bring you wonderful news.

A Savior has been born tonight

in Bethlehem!"

The shepherds looked in wonder
at the angel.

They were thinking,

"How shall we find this Savior?"

But the angel was saying,
"Look for a baby
wound all around in a cloth.
He is lying in a manger."

Then the sky was filled with angels.

"Glory to God," they sang

to the shepherds.

"Peace on earth to

everyone!"

Then the angels disappeared.

The shepherds rubbed their eyes.

"Come," one of them said.

"Let us go to Bethlehem!

Let us go and see

this little child!"

The shepherds hurried
down to Bethlehem.

They found the cave behind the inn.

They found the little Jesus

lying in the manger.

Quietly,

they bowed their heads

in prayer.

Then the shepherds left the cave.
They told the wonderful news
to everyone they met.

They told about the angel
who had said, "A Savior has been
born tonight in Bethlehem!"

ABOUT THE AUTHOR

Dorothy Van Woerkom is the author of five children's books. Her first, *Stepka and the Magic Fire,* received the Catholic Press Association award for best religious children's book of 1974. *Becky and the Bear,* a book for beginning readers, and *The Queen Who Couldn't Bake Gingerbread* were both Junior Literary Guild Selections. In addition to *Stepka,* Ms. Van Woerkom has written several other books for Concordia: *The Dove and the Messiah* and *Journeys to Bethlehem* for children, and a book of inspirational poetry for adults, *Wake Up and Listen.* She and her husband live in Houston.